THIS NOTEBOOK BELONGS TO

CONTACT

See our range of fine, illustrated books, ebooks, notebooks and art calendars:
www.flametreepublishing.com

This is a FLAME TREE NOTEBOOK
Published and © copyright 2018 Flame Tree Publishing Ltd

FTNB187 • 978-1-78755-026-1

THE
NATIONAL
GALLERY

Cover image based on
Ambrosius Bosschaert the Elder, 1573–1621
A Still Life of Flowers in a Wan-Li Vase (detail),1609–10
© The National Gallery, London. nationalgallery.org.uk
Produced and distributed under licence for the National Gallery, London, by Flame Tree Publishing Ltd

Ambrosius Bosschaert the Elder was a Dutch Golden Age painter. The flowers in this arrangement, which include lilies, tulips, roses, and carnations, are painted with almost scientific precision. Bosschaert's choice of a smooth copper support enhances the extraordinary detail of his brushwork. The bouquet itself, however, is a fiction: these flowers do not bloom at the same time, and would have been far too precious to cut for temporary display.

FLAME TREE PUBLISHING | The Art of Fine Gifts
6 Melbray Mews, London SW6 3NS, United Kingdom

All rights reserved. Printed in China. Created in the UK.